Echoes of my journey: Life in verse

Namrata S

BookLeaf Publishing

India | USA | UK

Presentation by *BookLeaf Publishing*

Web: www.bookleafpub.com

E-mail: info@bookleafpub.com

ISBN: 9789363310032

First edition 2024

I dedicate this book to the inner child we often forget and bury deep within—the innocence of the dreamer, now transformed into today's self-realized wisdom. May these poems serve as a reminder to honor that inner spark, cherish the inner child, and never lose sight of the dreams that shape us to be who we want to be.

ACKNOWLEDGEMENT

This collection of poems would not have been possible without the support and inspiration of many remarkable individuals who have encouraged me to reach within and beyond.

To all those who have left their mark on my life, from which I have risen to be who I am today—

To everyone in my family, friends, colleagues, acquaintances, strangers, who contributed to or crossed my life path.

PREFACE

It is in the quiet moments, when the noise of the day fades away, that I often find myself reflecting on the paths that I chose to walk on, the choices I've made, and the experiences that have shaped me. It is in these moments that I have found solace and inspiration in the form of poetry.

"Echoes of my journey: Life in verse" is born from these reflections. This collection is not just a series of poems but a heartfelt narrative of my life's journey—an amalgamation of emotions, thoughts, and experiences that have left an indelible mark on my soul. Each poem is a fragment of my story, a glimpse into the moments that have defined who I am today.

Writing these poems has been a deeply personal experience. It has allowed me to go deeper into my memories, to confront my fears, to celebrate my triumphs, and to embrace the entirety of my human experience. Through these poems, I have found the voice to the silent corners of my heart, to articulate the unsaid, and to share the beauty and pain of my journey with you.

As you read these poems, my hope is that you will find your own experiences mirrored within these verses. Each one of us is unique, and so is the path and our journey, but the emotions we feel and the challenges we face are universal. May these poems offer you comfort in times of sorrow, joy in moments of happiness, and a sense of connection in knowing that you are not alone in your experiences.

I invite you to join me on this poetic journey, to walk with me through the landscapes of memory, love, loss, and discovery and awareness. Let these poems be a bridge between us, a way to connect our hearts and minds through the timeless power of words.

Thank you for allowing me to share my story with you. May "Echoes of my journey: Life in verse" resonate with your own life's journey and inspire you to reflect on the beauty of your own story.

A fragment of my beginning

In eager breath, a speck of light I wait,
Whispering to the heavens, my soul's dictate.
In my promise, a pledge divine,
To love my Creator before mine.

With heart and soul, this vow I sign,
To cherish the Divine, for all time.
With divine's nod, light spreads its wings wide,
Guiding me forth on a celestial ride.

Amidst the chiming bells, I gently glide,
To be reborn, once more, by destiny's tide.
In the cradle of fate, I emerge anew,
Amidst tears and joy, a sight to imbue.

In the patriarchal fold, I open my eyes,
A girl amidst expectations and sighs.
In a world where norms decree my guise,
I ponder if innocence will suffice.

But laughter and song, my spirit's decree,
Amidst the shadows, I dance carefree.
A Laughing Buddha, born a girl, you see,
In this world, a soul set free.

Childhood whispers

In the garden of life, a new bud is born,
A tender shoot, a leaf adorned.
Through infancy's haze and toddler's stride,
Days drift by like a gentle tide.

Though siblings are grown and mother feels
strain,
Joy in the youngest remains a sweet refrain.
In scorching heat and amidst friends' laughter,
A child's heart finds joy ever after.

Roaming alone in nature's embrace,
Conversations with creatures, a sacred space.
Peacocks, ants, doves, and butterflies,
Whispers of innocence under open skies.

From root to leaf, a journey profound,
In childhood's realm, true happiness found.

Quest within

Who am I? What do I seek? Where does it
begin? Where does it lead?
Is it endless? And if it ends, when does it cease?

A mind quests for answers, forever asking,
Why not dwell in the present, feeling and
observing?

Fleeing the present, yet longing to stay,
Can I grasp it in the moment's sway?
For fear, it will vanish, slip away,
Leaving memories of yesterday.

Past and future, intertwined in flight
But where's the present, in full sight?
A place where senses awaken clear,
Listening closely to all that's near.

Healing through forgiveness

In the shadowed night, the girl stood alone,
scared and trembling,
Not knowing where to turn as figures emerged
from the dark, approaching.
Past midnight, her heart pounded, rooted in fear,
Yet providence watched over her as strangers'
paths drew near.

Seizing the moment, she led them cautiously,
Small hand Knocking on the door, a bit
hesitantly.
Standing there, unsure of what awaited,
Till kind hands and gentle eyes drew her inside.

Tears flowed freely as she found solace in the
haven,
A burden lifted, though another filled her heart.
A cozy bed and a warm embrace, the divine's
sign of love,
She drifted into sleep, the inner child scarred but
at peace.

Waking up, she realized this secret was to be
held within her deep,
Now a woman wiser, she made her peace with
the inner child's burden to keep.
Whose innocence had led her through.
With gentle strength, she embraced her past,
Letting go of herself, at long last.
For in forgiveness, there's healing's grace,
A tender embrace in love's embrace.

United they rise, stronger than before,
The woman and the child, forevermore.

Cherished melodies; shattered dreams

Running free on grass, under the open sky,
With friends, we laughed, reaching for fruits up
high.
Till dusk, we played, with joy and glee,
Seasons changed so did I; childhood slipped
away from me.

Becoming a young girl, innocence still in place,
Long hair flowing, with an innocent face.
Life's changes came, swift and bold,
As a new place beckoned, a story yet untold.

Leaving behind the grass, I felt a pang of loss,
In a city's center embrace, where concrete meets
moss.
Surrounded by faces, yet feeling alone,
In this urban jungle, a heart seeks its own.

Amidst the chaos, a rose in hand,
Offered by a boy whose intentions I couldn't
understand.
Confusion reigned as I turned away,
Unaware of the games that young hearts play.

Mercy of God, the school remained the same,
Young lads offering friendship, but I brushed off
their bold ways.
Until one day, a shout made me look back,
Eyes met, he blinked, and both of us smiled, off
track.

A knock in my heart, opening to let someone in,
Time stood still, as gazes locked in a spin.
But a handful of stolen moments soon turned
into a nightmare,
As he vanished like lightning, leaving me
exposed under everyone's glare

Alone, I bore the weight of misery's tide,
Heart bleeding in darkness, tears I couldn't hide.
Yet through the pain, a smile I'd feign,
As time passed, he appeared again.

In a state of turmoil, we held hands and wept,
Knowing all was nearing an end, our secrets
were kept.

For he was too young, unprepared for the
weight,
And I, not yet an adult, facing a different fate.

Alas, life's path led us in separate ways,
Yet memories lingered in the passage of days.
Life moved on, with glimpses of him often a
stride,
His eyes carrying the sadness of not being his
bride.

Echoes of clouded July

She asked the divine why are decisions so tough,
To keep or to let go, shouldn't be for us!
The agony of that day she could never forget,
As the sorrow still lives, never to beget.

The dull gray pouring from the sky,
In the holy month of clouded July,
The day so vividly etched in her heart,
As her soul shattered and fell apart.

For the weakness of us humans, one can't
describe,
For we keep false egos and misguided attitudes
most of our lives.
When the time comes to make a sound decision,

We look up to the divine for his holy
intervention.

The wrongs we do in our lives,
Never do we stand up and take it in stride.
Why do we think of others and their judgments,
When it's our lives, shouldn't we face the
consequences?

Decades have passed, but every July the day
beckons,
Reviving the same heaviness and wounds to
reopen.
But today, ready to accept and ask for
forgiveness from the divine,
As this is in memory of the lost bloodline.

Echoes of a free spirit

My free spirit has always taken me afar,
Terrains to climb and rivers to cross.
At an age when people partied hard,
I would pack fast to be under the stars.

The pearl-white snowy mountains,
The lush greens with the gushing fountains.
I feel the presence here all around,
Heart full of love and joy forever found.

The dark night, the fireflies, the forest's gentle
breeze,
Gazing at stars, listening to the river's melodies.
Far from the crowded world,
To just lay under the vastness, unfurled.

This is where truly my heart belongs,
For here there is no burden of duties prolonged.

Wandering in the forest, listening to the autumn leaves,
The sweet breeze that catches my breath and weaves.
Drinking from the river, the water cools my soul,
Splashing with hands, feeling perfectly whole.

I see the golden rays causing a halo,
For here our divine lives, free from sorrow.
The mystical valley's waiting for an embrace,
A place where my soul finds its grace.

Bearing light through the darkness

In the shadow of judgment, that word cut deep,
A painful reminder of wounds that bleed.

Despite my struggles alone, my tears hidden,
Me deemed unworthy and will be forbidden.

A threat given quietly, with nobody to hear,
When truth unfolded, I was held and thought to
be a liar.

I looked to my beloved to stand up for me,
But he lay quietly, unfazed by the scene

Lost in the darkness, I bore the weight
Of the cruel word, a burden of fate.

Two precious lives, lost in the fray,

How am I a "barren," I wondered day after day.

In the depths of despair, I searched for light,
For solace in the midst of the night.

But the word echoed loudly, tearing me apart,
A dagger to the soul, a stab piercing my heart.

Alone in my suffering, away from my roots,
My beloved, always fleeing uncaring, avoiding
disputes.

For in the depths of suffering, light can be
found,
My faith and prayers always lifting me from the
ground.

My biggest blessing

In the silence of surrender, after a decade's strife,
I laid down my burdens and surrendered my life.
To the one up above, I entrusted my plea,
For a gift beyond measure, I longed to see.

Through the trials endured and the tears I shed,
I learned to let go and to trust instead.
In the stillness of faith, I found my release,
And surrendered my dreams to the hands of
peace.

Then, like a whisper, a gentle reply,
A miracle bestowed from the depths of the sky.
A beautiful baby boy, fair and handsome skin
like ruby,
A blessing from God meant just for me.

In his eyes, I saw hope; in his smile, I found
grace,
A symbol of love in this sacred space.
For in the moment of surrender, I found my joy,
In the precious gift of my beautiful baby boy.

A decade of waiting, a journey so long,
Yet in God's perfect timing, I found where I
belong.
For He heard my prayers, in the depths of
despair,
And blessed me with a miracle beyond compare.

Istanbul: A heavenly note

In the land of dervishes, their twirls a sacred
dance,
Skirts swirling like the dome of mosques in
trance.
The night view from atop the hill, a breathtaking
sight,
A thousand candles on water, glowing in the
night.

Istanbul lives in two, divided by the blue,
Of Bosphorus waters, a timeless view.
Ferries gently sway, calling those in haste,
To cross to the other side, with no time to waste.

Calls from the minarets, divine in their sound,
A reminder of faith, ever profound.
Eight years in Istanbul, life's lyrical song,
Even in hardship, it never felt wrong.

Far from our families, but dreamlike it seemed,
Life in Istanbul, just like we dreamed.
Struggles were lighter by the seaside's grace,
Beckoning us to pour worries into its embrace.

Some sip in cafes, a serene retreat,
While others stride with purpose to the jobs they
greet.
Newspapers flutter as tea cups lie,
Seagulls go wild for bagels thrown high.

We crossed each bridge that life threw our way,
Personal or professional, we found our sway.
Every place has its magic and in Istanbul's
charms,
We found solace and peace in its loving arms.

Trials and turbulence, always close by,
But the highs of Istanbul let our spirits fly.
In the beauty of this city, our hearts found rest,
Istanbul, forever, our lives it blessed.

Pursuit for self

In the depths of my soul, shadows dwell,
A silent symphony, an untold tale.
Whispers of doubt, echoes of fear,
In the labyrinth of self, I draw near.

Roots unseen yet deeply entwined,
Identity's puzzle, intricately designed.
In search of truth, I journey within,
Exploring the depths where doubts begin.

With each heartbeat, a symphony of choice,
I raise my voice, drowning the noise.
In the silence of truth, I find my song,
Amidst the tumult, where I belong.

In the silence of my heart, whispers stir,
A journey within, seeking what's unsure.
Amidst confusion, I find my way,
With faith as my guide, I embrace it anyway.

Oh, boundless Universe, in your vast space,
Guide me with wisdom through this unknown
place.
Through doubts and questions, clarity I pursue,
Finding peace in truths, accepting what is true.

Divine yearning

Oh, Divine, your presence I seek,
In strangers' eyes, I find but mere mystique.
Why do you hide from me, deny your grace?
Without you near, life's meaning I cannot
embrace.

I sense you in every soul I meet,
In their laughter, in their silent retreat.
You've woven us together, a tapestry divine,
Now let your light upon me shine.

To you, I wish to pour my heart's song,
To sit at your feet, where I belong.
To serve and care for you, my deepest desire,
In your presence, my soul shall never tire.

Grant me not just visions in my mind,
But your touch, your voice, so kind.
Let me rest my head upon your gentle lap,
As your words like pearls, my spirit unwraps.

Souls of stars

On New Year's Eve, she saw his stars and
constellation,
She whispered, "For your life, avoid tonight's
intoxication,"

She kept urging, he kept listening close,
Yet in between, softly opposing, she supposed.

Tonight's the night he said, let me be merry and
sip,
She feared, if he did, the year ahead would slip.

You're the master of your mind, she said, let it
be,
He relented, no drinks tonight, just let me be
free.

She sat and prayed, listening to the hymns,
The divinity of the holy place, her soul in it
swims.

In the gentle whispers of the sacred air,
She found solace, releasing every care.

Seeking forgiveness for his wrongs, wishes for
his joy,
Leaving the rest to God, their souls to deploy.

All night, lingering thoughts filled her mind,
Wondering what he's doing, what he'd find.

Less of his voice, more of the written,
In distant places, love is often bitten.

Past midnight, the ringing startled her,
She looked at the name, and everything went
blur.

Her heart raced as she answered the call,
In a trembling laugh, she stood, unsteady, ready
to fall.

Inebriated, he wished her for the new year with
cheer,
And in the same breath, though mumbled, his "I
love you" was so clear.

She froze; time seemed to stand still,
heartbeats syncing, as if by will.
What he felt, she seemed to hear,
Lost in his voice, she held dear.

So much understood, without a word to say,
Their hearts intertwined, in their own way.
This is the perfect beginning to a beautiful story,
Don't take it to heart, for no love sees its glory.

Echoes of souls

Thee became a part of thou, a thought
unimagined,
Within him, she thought she'd find solace, a
dream unforeseen.

In each other's embrace, they'd build the nest,
like a dream unfurled,
But reality razed their dream home, leaving her
adrift in this world.

Now she sits, homeless, seeking traces of their
lost abode,
Once their sanctuary, now estranged, a path they
never rode.

It wasn't a house of bricks, but dreams they
wove,
Yet tears gave it substance, a reality they never
strove.

Resting on his chest, once dwelling, now a
memory stained,
Forever etched in her heart, the loss, the pain
unchained.

Though the souls met, destiny kept them apart, a
fate unforeseen,
In the collision of their dreams and reality, their
love was deemed.

Yet in this saga of love and loss, a poignant truth
remains unsaid,
In the theatre of reality, they were mere
spectators, their paths never led.

Life's full circle

In the dances of love, hope's tender glow,
Promises are made, emotions flow.
But darkness lurks, betrayals ring
Happiness fleeting, heartache's sting.

Through trials deep, my spirit grew,
Learning truths both old and new.
Love's sweet song, a fleeting tune,
Betrayed by lies beneath the moon.

Yet from the pain, I found my grace,
Learning to heal, finding my place.
In paths of light, where hope persists,
I embrace the journey, scars, and twists.

Now a healer's path I tread,
With wisdom gleaned from tears once shed.
Love's lessons etched upon my soul,
Finding peace, making me whole.

Shadows of Betrayal

I was broken and hurt, living in the dark when
we met,
He pushed me to be free, flying out, not fearing
the net.

I took the path, scared, holding his hand,
Unaware, he too was hurting and inside snapped.

We tried to be present, but past took precedence,
his and mine,
Somehow picking our pieces, together we
mended, entwined.

He found me, and I stepped again, little knowing
into the dark,
Others came in too soon between us, the young
ones, especially the widow on the yacht.

Praising her in front of me, making me feel so
small,
He being my beloved and I his wife, said a few
words to befall.

The stinging on my cheeks, heavy on me now
dawned,
I regretted not listening to my father, whose
foresight was so strong for he had said,

"Darling daughter, there's no shame in retracing
your steps,
As no promises have been made so far."

But I was so in love and blind, as they say,
I didn't see my fate taking a leap into the holy
fire of the "seven steps" away.

I was taunted and made fun of, but I heard it all,
For I was in love and couldn't take this fall.

My mother and father shouldn't suffer for my
wrong decisions,
I pulled myself and smiled, devoid of any
suspicions.

For a father can see his daughter's heart cry,
God took him within a year, and my heart tore,
saying the last goodbye.

My life became something I had not anticipated,
The whole world turned upside down and
became complicated.

Life, happiness, peace, laughter slipped away
like sand,
Holding fear, anxiety, pain, and my little son in
my hand.

Abandoned for five days by him, something died
inside,
They all blamed me, and not even one tried to
console me or hold me tight.

Only my roots bore the weight of my grief,
Mother, sister, brother, and son were the only
ones left with me.

Broken, I welcomed him back, unaware this was
all planned,
Shaken to the core, color started fading off my
body as my mind went blank.

How much do I share with you all,
For he and his clan easily malign me, for I not
the daughter but the daughter-in-law.

The stinging of slaps and gasping of breath,
what all do I hide or share,
The hurt and pain as yet again you betray.

My father was right in saying, for any broken
girl, will he get easily swayed,
I am tired of waiting with bated breath, what's
next today?

I let go of him as he is already taken for the last
decade,
By the same one in the past who had him
broken, and now me betrayed.

This is my life, and I must stand up, not even
fully healed,
For my womb's been taken and left me weak.

I believe in God Almighty and His decisions,
Nobody can ruin me, for I am my own
inspiration.

Rising from the ashes

In life's vast symphony of highs and lows,
We find ourselves amid the ebb and flow.

When shadows loom and darkness creeps,
We gather strength, though our spirit weeps.

Like the phoenix, from ashes, we rise,
Defying odds, reaching for the skies.

For in every trial, a lesson is found,
A chance to grow, to stand our ground.

The rose, with petals soft and fair,
Bears thorns that pierce, yet beauty it shares.

In life's garden, amidst pain and woe,
We learn to bloom, despite the throe.

Do thorns protect or pose a threat?
In their embrace, resilience we beget.

For failures, like thorns, remind us true,
To cherish each moment, each sky of blue.

So let us embrace life's twists and turns,
For in every challenge, a lesson we learn.

With courage and faith, we'll weather the storm,
And emerge victorious in our life's reform.

Fleeting whispers

Today, yet another day tiptoed into her thoughts,
Each word of his, a poignant touch to her heart it
brought,

What is this, why this blend of love and strife?
Understanding, she has urged her heart to
embrace this life.

He held her close, unsettling, yet in her mind's
embrace,
Let's treasure these moments, finding solace in
their grace.

Their bond transcends time... love's depth then,
echoes today,
It was known, to meet yet remain apart, they'd
have to sway.

Embracing the truth, even if they meet, they'll
keep a distance,
The essence was to sense each other's existence,

No complaints, whether something befell or not,
Love, from afar, profound and complete, their
hearts have wrought.

Perhaps this love wasn't confined to the day's
sun's arc,
But spans through lifetimes, an eternal spark.

The dawning

With each fall, I rise from ashes, broken yet
resilient,
Piece by piece, I rebuild my life amidst intrusion
and ruin.

Why, oh why, do I endure this relentless
torment?
It shatters me, pierces me, yet I return to the
same lament.

Surely, destiny holds a brighter path for me,
Yet my own brokenness seems to summon more
agony.

I must soar beyond this cycle of suffering,
seeking solace within,

How long can I bear such sorrow, seeking
fleeting joy in borrowed moments thin?

For every wound inflicted because of them,
I summon a smile, with each pain I endure, I
nurture my strength.
Letting tears fall, a pool of empathy, a beacon of
grace,
For you, my beloved, finding solace
In love's embrace
But I am not made for this suffocation, my heart
finds no place.

This is not the end, but a new dawn I see
A rebirth, another beginning, a journey to set
myself free.

Scars and stars

In the depths of my soul, anguish resides,
Not forlorn love's absence, but human tides.

Eyes entwine with mine, spinning webs of
deceit,
As if truth were but a fanciful feat.

Falsehoods, secrets, betrayal, their constant
refrain,
Rending trust a fragile, shattered chain.

Your apathy, a silent, haunting call,
Leaving scars where trust once stood tall.

Why pretend normalcy when turmoil brews
inside?
This disrespect, this disregard, I cannot abide.

Yet amidst the wreckage, a prophecy unfolds,
Of endings, beginnings, stories yet untold.

The old slips away, like sand through hands,
New beginnings beckon across distant lands.

Gather courage, gather strength, forge anew,
In the wake of pain, find hope true.

Divine reverence

In the realm where faith does reign,
I walk the path, untouched by pain.
Beneath your watchful, guiding hand,
I find the strength to firmly stand.

With every chant, I feel you near,
Your presence soothing, crystal clear.
For every wrong, I seek your grace,
In humble reverence, I find my place.

Blessed with a family, steadfast and true,
In times of trial, they see me through.
Abundance of joy, love's endless embrace,
Each blessing cherished, each moment's grace.

In every heartbeat, your blessings shine,
Fulfilling wishes, dreams align.
A tapestry of grace, woven with care,
In your divine light, I find solace everywhere.

Forgiveness

Forgiveness embraces the hurt and anger,
Choosing to heal and finding peace thereafter.
But it doesn't mean we erase the memory,
Or pretend the pain never came to be.

It's about understanding and moving on,
Learning from what happened, though it's gone.
The scars remind us of lessons learned,
While forgiveness grows and hearts are turned.

In forgiving, we reclaim our power,
To shape the present, to face the hour.
To cherish wisdom from the past's embrace,
Where forgiveness and remembrance both
remain.

So, forgive to set yourself free,
But remember to learn from what you see.
Letting go doesn't mean you forget,
It means you choose to move forward, no regret.

Sacred Reflections

In the cold, misty, quiet night
We whisper to ourselves
Wrapped tightly in our embrace
We visit you each year

Stepping into the cold water's embrace
I glimpse the golden shine
Amid winter night's darkness
Under the moon's silver light

The lake's gentle ripples
Echo the hymns' melody
Through the air, I breathe
Sacred tears shed

In your comforting embrace
Heart brimming with gratitude
I delve deep within, quiet
My soul peacefully in solitude

Dreams

In the twinkling depths of night, my dreams
unfold,
Where whispers of stars blow dust of gold
In realms of my unseen open eyes,
Where reality's grasp gently unties.

Through hazy mists, I wander far,
Chasing shiny dust of a distant star.
In fields of lavender and moonlit streams,
Where reality melts into surreal dreams.

Dancing with shadows, I fly so high,
Through the painted skies, where silence lies.
In the embrace of whispered sighs,
Where the heart finds solace under midnight
skies.

But dawn's gentle rays fall on my face,
Breaking the spell of night's trace.
Yet memories linger, faint and sweet,
Of a dreamer's journey in realms complete.

True Passion

In melodies of childhood's song,
Where peacocks danced, I did belong.
Curiosity led me far and wide,
Not knowing what makes my spirit bright.

Friends, acquaintances' words like gentle wind,
Showed paths where joy resides within.
Imagining days filled with delight,
In passions found, my heart takes flight.

For in the quest to find my place,
I found my passion's steady embrace.
A journey etched with joy and pain,
Yet never shall I search in vain.

Though doubts may linger, I stand tall,
Courageous steps, I heed the call.
Exploring paths, both near and far,
I find my passion, like a guiding star.

Seeds of Intentions

In the dark stillness of the night,
Weaving intentions, undenied.
On the fabric, a grand design,
I etch it deep in my mind.

Waking up on, opening my eyes,
I feel the nudge from inside.
Clear as crystal, like the morning dew,
Goals take shape, ambitions true.

With courage held and spirit bright,
Intentions glow in gentle light.
On a canvas, blank and new,
To paint with hopes, steadfast and true.

Like seeds in spring, intentions sown,
In fertile soil, they steadily grow.
With each day's grace and gentle flow,
A brighter path begins to show.

A daughter's father

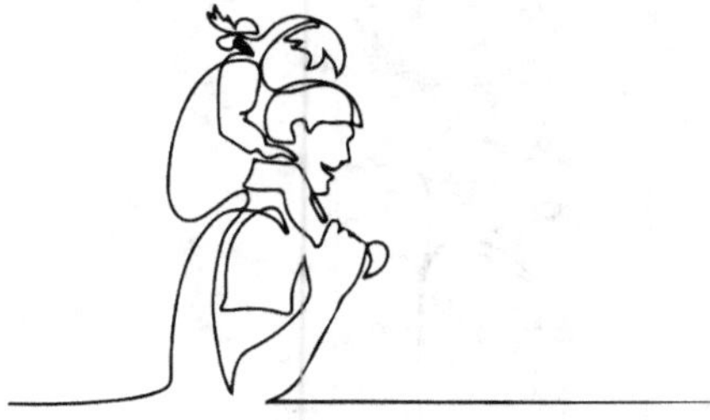

My earliest memories of my father,
Who loved me most,
For I was his sweet little one, always starry-eyed
and lost.
With four decades between us, he indulged my
whims and fuss,
Spoiled to the core, my wishes always fulfilled,
Never heeding his wisdom back then, now I
grasp its true essence.
His thoughts and foresight were so worldly wise,
If only I could share another sunrise.

He always encouraged me to be a woman of
substance,
To be different, not swayed by customs.
Throwing caution to the wind, I chose a path
different from his vision,
As I strayed from my dreams, I felt the pain he
held for me.

Who else but a father gives a life-lifting hug and hopes anew,
For better days to come, if only I would listen to his cue.
The words of wisdom that fell on deaf ears,
Every time I sought love from elsewhere.
Barely three decades with me, I lost him forever,
Now I look up at the stars with misty eyes,
whispering, "Come on, POPCORN, show the path and guide."
For no man is like a daughter's father,
That's why it's said, when a father's gone, a daughter's left without her secure shelter.

We the trio

A mother who is more like a sister, also my
friend,
A sister who loves me like her daughter, who
stood strong to defend.
Blessed to have both in my life's arc,
Close as can be, not even a breath could pass.

Through ups and downs, both held my hand
tight,
One heard my pain, the other calmed my mind.
Love binding our hearts, forging forever,
Once the three musketeers, mischief makers,
today laughter we endeavor.

Gratitude I give for the love they bestow,
For within this circle, my heart finds its glow.
If reborn, I pray to divine, bless me the same,
To keep this bond unbroken, our special infinite
love chain.

Flowing colorways

Vibrant colors, alive and bold,
They beckon me to join their fold.
With swirls and strokes, from void, they rise,
Emotions turbulent, yet on canvas they
harmonize.

Dancing to melodies of hues so bright,
Smooth as velvet, yet rough in their might.
Brush bristles glide, like a gentle caress,
Blurring, merging, emotions confess.

My pain dissolves in this palette divine,
Brush laid down, I witness beauty shine.
Signing my name, where emptiness lies,
A creation born from heart, not mind.

My life in a verse

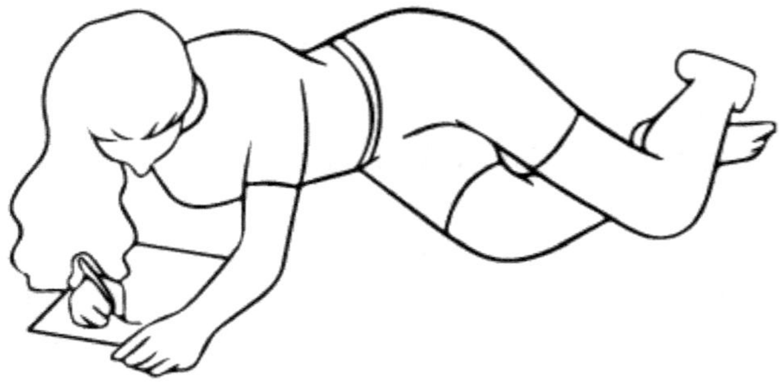

Once upon a time, a young girl crafted her own
rhymes,
Impressed by her talent, her father gifted a diary
and a pen,
"Capture your thoughts, let your imagination
soar,"
He encouraged, "Your journey begins, embrace
what's in store."

With just a few words to lines, she scribbled
with glee,
Though young and inexperienced, she yearned
to be free.
Years drifted by, gathering tales far and wide,
Supported by loved ones, her story awaited its
stride.

Unsure where to start, unsure how to write,
A dream nudged her, guiding her path through
the night,
From caterpillar to cocoon, then a butterfly's
flight,
People tried but couldn't pen her tale quite right.

Divine intervention unveiled a new twist,
"You'll write your own story, using words that
persist,"
Not just in words, but in prose she found,
Guided gently, her pen danced to the sound.

But the tale doesn't end with this final verse,
New beginnings beckon, a story yet to traverse.

Echoes of procrastination

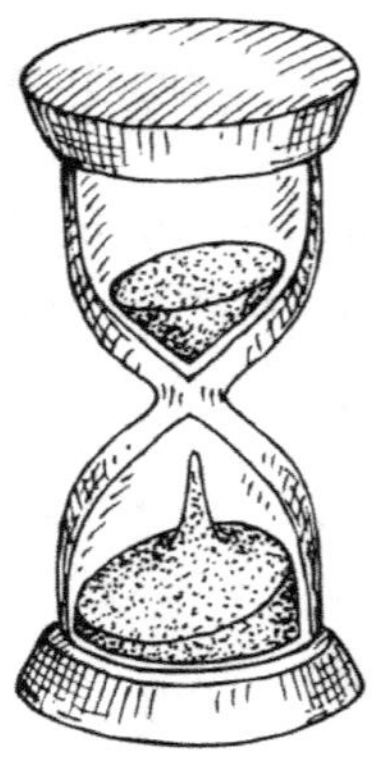

In shadows deep, where time stands still,
Dwadling weaves its will,
A quiet thief of fleeting grace,
It steals the moments we embrace.

Tasks loom large with promises unkept,
Dreams deferred where hopes have slept,
Yet in this pause, a restless mind,
Finds solace in the chains it binds.

The hours drift on lazy streams,
Lost in half-formed, idle dreams,
A future awaits, a distant shore,
It now remains a closing door.

In gentle whispers, it deceives,
With idle pleasures, it conceives,
A fleeting comfort in delay,
The price of now, we'll dearly pay.

So break the spell, reclaim the day,
For time once lost won't find its way,
In action's light, the fears dissolve,
And from the depths, solutions evolve.

Rain's embrace

Penning down thoughts, I stare through my
window,
Blue sky and white clouds like cotton softly laid.
The sun's warmth beads on my brow,
Lost in my work, my mind in its own parade.

A dark shadow drifts in, and I gaze up in awe,
Black clouds tumble like lovers in a squall.
Thunder's deep growl stirs the air with its might,
As rain whispers down, reshaping the light.

From gloom arises beauty, fresh and profound,
Stepping into the rain, each drop a soft sound.
Like water soothing a parched throat, calming
and sweet,
Arms open I dance like a peacock, in blissful
trance on my feet.

The flowers and leaves seem to awaken anew,
With every drop, my heart dances with delight.
In the rain's embrace, my spirit feels true,
A symphony of joy in the storm's soft light.

The last of us

I am the generation of modern times,
Preserving the values, welcoming the new.
We honor our culture and adapt with the climb,
Balancing both, a blend that is true.

Yet, as I look around at the rapid pace,
It feels like we're losing ourselves in the fray.
I recall days spent in parks, meals with family
full of grace,
Summers with grandmother, waiting for our
stay.

Climbing trees for fruit, pulling sugar cane,
The gardener's chase, a playful refrain.
We had siblings aplenty, a lively crew,
Now parents plan for one, a shift in view.

We shared our triumphs, our losses alike,
Now technology dominates, and connections
strike.
Children, pampered and pushed through the
grind,
Carefree days replaced by endless grind.

Sometimes I wonder what they truly gain,
But I know well what they've lost in the chain.
In echoes of the past, a truth is clear,
A simpler joy, now distant but dear.

Mind's triumph

Though the journey's been rocky and steep,
And more often than not, felt the feeling of
defeat,
Each trial and challenge faced
Was a lesson learned, never erased.

The past may shape but doesn't confine,
It's a guide, a shining light, a sign,
To help me through life's winding way,
And uncover strength with each new day.

So I'll take charge and rewrite my fate,
Turning each setback into something great.
For every hurdle, I've managed to clear
Was a stepping stone to something near.

Let purpose lead with every stride,
And let my story be one of pride.
For every moment that came before
Prepared me for what's in store.

I'll release the pain, the hurt, the strain,
Embrace the lessons and let joy reign.
My story is far from being done,
With the conviction, life's meaningful moments
are yet to come.

Verses: A Life unfolded

To write my own life story in verse
I wandered through time's embrace,
To relive moments of joy and sorrow,
And trace the contours of my place.

With a blank canvas in hand,
Memories unfolded with each stroke,
As the quill dances over the page,
A vivid tale begins to evoke.

Childhood days emerged in vibrant hues,
Friends, plays, fights brightly recalled,
The paths we roamed and dreams we chased,
In those early moments, enthralled.

Teenage years unfolded with fervent dreams,
A blend of hope and bold rebellion,
Crushes and the stirrings of defiance,
Marking the age of my own expansion.

Young adulthood's journey takes its course,
Choices carved and lessons embraced,
Wisdom gleaned from trials faced,
And triumphs earnestly placed.

Now, as the final lines are drawn,
And the story finds its grace,
The essence of a life well lived
Unfolds in each carefully penned space.

With this chapter gently closing,
The essence of who I've become shines,
Embracing the lessons and the roads ahead,
In the journey that intertwines.

Beyond the tears

In the quiet hollow of a broken heart,
Where echoes of lost love and sorrow start,
A poet is born not in the midst of cheer,
But from the shards of pain, so crystal clear.

Through nights of yearning and days of despair,
In every breath, the weight of love laid bare,
The lines emerge, like whispers in the night,
Of snatched dreams and hearts yearning to unite.

The lover's journey does not cease,
In the echo of a love with no peace,
For in the depths of grief and longing's woe,
A greater truth begins to softly show.

From the ashes of a lover's mournful plea,
A poet rises, unchained and free,
Understanding that the heart must mend,
To craft the verse that guides, transcends.

In letting go of love's forlorn embrace,
The soul finds space for wisdom's grace,
And through the pain that once had bound the
pen,
Emerges a voice that speaks to all again.

So from the torn and weary lover's plight,
A true poet finds their voice, their light,
For in the journey of loss and release,
Comes the birth of verse and profound peace.

A new legacy: Dark shadows to bright light

In days of old, our societal beliefs
Offered little hope for girls, causing them grief.
Struggling to voice their desires and dreams,
Bound by customs, unable to reject marriage
extremes.

Parents burdened by societal views,
Wondering why suffer, what's the excuse?
Creator made both girl and boy the same,
Yet one faced darkness, while the other gained
fame.

A daughter's birth seemed burdened with debts,
While a son's arrival was celebrated, no regrets.
He would carry the family name with pride,

Yet the woman who bore him was often
sidelined.

Marriage became a realm of decree,
Where a boy's wealth or learning defined what
could be.
But times have changed, awareness seeping
through,
Old ways fading as the new generation grew.

In four decades' span, my son and I reside,
With views evolving, progressive as our guide.
I wish for him to honor, not undermine,
The strength and wisdom in women, pure and
fine.

For I am not raising him just to be a son,
But to be a husband and father, second to none.
With respect as his guide and love as his creed,
To honor and cherish, and in every deed,

To value and uplift the women in his life,
With empathy and kindness, free from strife.
In these roles, he'll grow, and with wisdom, he'll
see,
The strength and the power in true equality.

She is: A woman of substance

Woman of substance
In the sacred realm of existence, where divinity meets the human,
She is the closest to the divine,
A vessel of life and boundless strength,
For nine months she carries the promise of tomorrow,
Enduring the profound ache of creation.

Her body bears the sacred burden,
Each pang a testament to her unwavering will,

In the act of giving life, she transcends,
With courage unmatched, through pain, she
emerges.

Yet her journey is marred by shadows,
Violence and discrimination, a relentless storm,
From the hands of men and, sorrowfully, her
own kind,
A woman, at times, becomes her own adversary,
In a twisted dance of progress and regression.

Each step she takes is on rugged terrain,
From birth to twilight, her path is fraught with
trials,
Yet it is her endurance that defines her,
Her resilience that carves her place in the
cosmos,
A beacon of strength and substance,
A testament to the indomitable spirit of
womanhood.